T0374104

"Catching a Glimpse"

Donald Davis

Copyright © 2015 by Donald Davis. 725786

ISBN: Softcover   978-1-5144-1561-0
         Hardcover   978-1-5144-1562-7
         EBook   978-1-5144-1560-3

All rights reserved. No part of this book may
be reproduced or transmitted in any form or by
any means, electronic or mechanical, including
photocopying, recording, or by any information storage
and retrieval system, without permission in writing from
the copyright owner.

Print information available on the last page

Rev. date: 10/27/2015

To order additional copies of this book, contact:
Xlibris
1-888-795-4274
www.Xlibris.com
Orders@Xlibris.com

ABOUT THE BOOK:

CATCHING A GLIMPSE" (Glimpse: A brief or partial view)

"WHAT CAN I TELL YOU?

My book is an array of Glimpses that I have written in many formats for the past three decades. Since I prefer short-succinct reports, I have begun with a Haiku Style. Haiku is quite new to me and tells a story briefly. It has to be brief since I usually limit myself to just 17 syllables per offering. Here is an example:

Shopping for produce, (5)
grabbing a handful of grapes (7)
Hands slapped by small kids. (5).... Syllables

It kind of hangs together, may have a message or some fun and maybe some sadness.

I have incuded quite a few family stories. I notice that I like stories with animals, who are on center stage or bit players.Watch for a peacock, dogs or horses. .Other characters are also in the mix. I've taken some liberties with Odes and Ballads. There may be a traditional poem or two.. Some of my relatives-Names changed- are here. I'm here too. Best wishes.

1. HAIKU 5-7-5

A. "Breathe in, out, hold it."

> "Breathe in, out, hold it."
> Doctor humming soft rock.
> Patient turning blue.

B. Yolk of life may spill

> Yolk of life may spill
> into nothingness or joy.
> Destiny beckons.

C. Songbird sings in flight

> Songbird sings in flight,
> or safely caged; no struggle
> Which path do we choose?

D. Bees trapeze on leaves

> Bees trapeze on leaves.
> Posies open for orgy.
> Warm honey drips joy.

E. Cop's Car

> Cop's car, Blue light-Stop!
> Bladder full, must relieve self
> Don't know where to turn

F. Blue Elephants Waltz

> Blue Elephants Waltz
> Purple Mice search for dance cards
> Sci-Fi Block Party

G. Sci-Fi baby speaks:

Sci-Fi baby speaks,
"I must have new smart phone now"
High Gluten Alert!

H. Cat Burglar unmasked

Cat Burglar unmasked
Same feline face is revealed
Front page, Sci-Fi Scoop

I. Imagine

Unicorns frolic
While reciting Dr. Seuss.
New world peace prevails.

J. What Next

I dive in the pool
To retrieve phone and hair piece
Loose shorts fly away

K. ANOTHER DAY (More Haiku-Style)

Calf invisible,
Unseen by slaughter- butchers
Graze another day.

L. Love, it's ME

"Hello Love, it's me."
"Wait, Who is this? Who are you?"
Alzheimer's: No Fun.

M. HORSE SENSE

Horse smiles; Kind brown eyes.
Come let us ride and be one
On our life long path.

N. Kitty and I:

We discussed our plight;
Then we promised to obey
our serious pledge.

Cat stalked a robin
I slandered a few neighbors
Today in Facebook.

What now furry feline?
Song birds and robins beware
Promises broken.

O. Beth and Hen

Beth, you smile-reach out.

Your Hen's gaze hangs on to your love.

Compassion for Two

2. FAMILY

A . FATHERLESS

June 16, 2014

Another Father's Day went by yesterday and I'm feeling more fatherless than ever.

FATHER-LESS- DADDY-LESS- DAD-LESS

Have I ever really seen you, except for that hidden wedding picture I found many years ago? It must have been more than seventy years. (Could I have been 'hiding' somewhere in that classic picture?-You know what I mean.)

"What a handsome guy," those special few tell me, with whom I share that special part of my life.

Yes, you were a handsome guy, Dad.

I heard you were pretty thin on top, so I can't describe that part of you. You were wearing one of those classy top-hats and it added to your allure. Everyone had to love your bright toothsome smile, dimpled chin and brilliant brown eyes. As far as I know, that brown eyes gene stopped with us, you and me, thank you.

I am sad and feel kind of empty when I reflect how your life was cancelled by the rest of the family whenever I asked about you. Just because you left, you became a non-person.

When did I really see you last? When I did, whether it was in a dream or a real life snapshot, I got off of my blue little threewheeler bike one cloudy day in New York City. You walked toward me and patted my head and hardly smiled. "Goodbye, Donnie" you said softly.

You were wearing a gray Fedora hat and carrying a cardboard looking suitcase. A soft, kind aura surrounded you. I don't remember feeling anything as I went back to my bicycle and met with a friend.

I didn't miss missing you then as I do now. Yet, it is nice to finally be in touch.

Happy Father's Day, Dad, for the first time, wherever you are.

My love to you,

B. Family: LAST NIGHT'S PERFUME

Narrated, in part, by Clara Gnatowsky, daughter of Momma Minnie, and, eventually, my mother.

1920's

LAST NIGHT'S PERFUME

7 am this morning.

Momma Minnie's song begins early this morning: "I'll be loving you, always, with a love that's true,, always."

"It was.hours ago when she tiptoed past my room, dressed like a Czarina. The stockings she wore are now wrinkle- wrapped around her ankles, leaving a few inches of tanned skin between them and the black velvety robe tied tightly around her diminutive, yet wonderfully sculpted body.

I park next to my pulpy orange juice, coffee and hot cereal and join her in song: "When the things you planned, need a helping hand." I get up and let her lead a lilting waltz; "I will understand, always."

"Hey, very good Clara! You know the words and you're extra light on your feet."

"For a kid my size, right? So you had a good time at your,um-uuh, meeting last night, Momma?" Minnie squints and cocks her head.

Minnie says, "Get ready for school. Your giggling girl friends will be calling soon. Come home early for your music lesson. Professor Axelrod charges from the time he opens the door, whether you are here or not. Thirty cents for not even an hour buys a lot of hot cereal. You know you should really put on that girdle I got you and pull the stockings up tight, if you please. Check your hair and fingernails too. Maybe Papa will come by later. You know how he is with the personal inspections."

"Papa is becoming a stranger, especially when you're around, Momma." I felt the throat- choking burn and blurted, "I think it's the other way around too."

"That's enough already!" Her tremolo jumps to strident string-plucking staccatos. A jagged beam darkens the liquid in her eyes, then the fitful sigh, the shaking head and a hasty peek at me. Softness returns. "I think I hear your friends. Oh, I'm staying at Aunt Shirley's tonight so I'll see you some time tomorrow." Momma's full mouth goodbye kiss is much more vibrant than ceremonial this morning: So was the hug she gave me outside the door. My friends applauded the scene and greeted Momma buoyantly;

"Hello Mrs. G." Momma waved.

While we walked to the bus stop, Momma's second song of the morning, more up tempo, washed past the darkened stucco exterior of our old two family house. "Everybody loves my baby, but my baby don't love nobody, but me"(Jack Palmer and Spencer Williams-1924) . . There was an elegant confidence in the air.

My High School friends marveled at 'Mrs. G's' freeing liberal spirit and openness: How willing she was to actively do what she believed for the poor, the socially downtrodden and women. Momma was likely sun worshipping on the roof in the buff, still humming as we crossed the street. Later, she'd be bathed, powdered and perfumed, her blonde natural curls glowing from the hundred brushings, her youthful body, well exercised and adorned with just enough flair. The pince-nez, attached to some lagniappe, would be resting on her bosom. Maestoso! Majestic! Oh, Papa, if you could see her now!

Papa (Sam): Fun, generous, sometimes imperious with us; A free spirit, yet a serious card player; A "man's man" at the pinochle table or the business meeting, "a lady's man" at social or other engagements; Always buffed and pressed from the fingertips to the wardrobe; Not a tee shirt and shorts guy, he always had a subtle barber shop aroma encircling him. A ubiquitous, albeit aromatic, cigar was gently clenched in his front teeth..I had a special love for Papa.

My friend, Ethel, gently elbowed my shoulder as we looked for a seat on the city bus. "You have that teary smile, Clara. Something about Momma and Papa, maybe?" she said. I blinked and nodded, freeing myself of the lingering reflections.

It must have been those insecurities provoked by my overgenerous girth that perpetuated my want or need to please others. Since I didn't have much money-who did? I'd entertain. My ploy worked on many levels. For now, my Minnie and Sammy G stories (Momma and Papa) kept my friends hanging on, waiting for the next installment. Most of our gang was in Advanced Senior English Class. When we were studying Edgar Allan Poe, parodies of Minnie and Sammy G prevailed: I recall this one:

It was many a year ago In a (N.Y.) kingdom by the sea
That a couple got hitched, whom you may know
They were Minnie and Sammy G.
He was a child and she was a child
In this kingdom by the sea
But they loved with a love that was more than a love;
Minnie and Sammy G.
Soon their love produced daughters three
Who grew up nice as could be
Then, broken became that golden bowl
Their love nest flown, Let the bells toll.
Minnie's tempting Axelrod to do her musical scales
Sammy's squeeze is Miss Louise
The babe who buffs his nails.

The next time I saw Momma and Papa in the same room together was just before the wedding.

Early '30s Clara narrates:

My kid sister, Becky, the shapely aggressive one, worthy of a racy biography, found a guy on Wall Street whose strings she could pull. Marriage talk was no secret. Laura, the baby, was busy doing summer stock musicals and singing jobs in speak- easy cabarets during the winter. Sammy was a chemist without portfolio, converting water and other choice ingredients into potable, albeit not legal, alcoholic beverages. He had a high-class bathtub operation and was well "protected." Minnie was active in the Socialist Party, charitable organizations and submitting romantic and protest poetry to newspapers and magazines. Both maintained rather active but reasonably discreet romances. Staten Island was a pretty small town in New York City.

I was working in Manhattan in a publishing house, partying, puffing cigarettes and fooling around with whatever and whomever was available. I was told by some that I wasn't a bad looker, maybe they had too much to drink. I could sing and dance all night and go to work fresh in the morning. I was always available to listen and use my sensitivity and sense of humor to great avail. I still had that need to entertain.

One early summer night, I was walking home from the bus stop. The barbershop and cigar mix in the air was unmistakable.

There he was, Papa, sitting on the front porch, dressed and shining as usual. His being there, especially this time, was not typical. Neither was an initial tone of reluctance in his voice. He didn't even give me the obvious quick inspection.

Papa spoke, "Clara, you know Becky and Dave want to be married soon." I half smiled and nodded. He was warmed up now and more in command: "I know you're out with this one and that one. It's OK, you are a grown lady."

I thought; "Spare me the 'facts of life" routine, please Papa. I wasn't crazy about the 'grown lady' part either.

"Well, he said, anyway, Minnie and I were talking ('Hey that's good.') and we want you to meet a nice boy." ('Hey, that's..') Maybe we can have a double wedding." All of that followed by half a hug, a quick kiss on the lips and tender smile. Papa means business!

"Maybe.! " Papa says. (Sure! 'Maybe.') " I bet Papa, with his extensive customer base, has already made reservations with Lefkowitz, the Caterer, O'Neill, who runs the wedding hall and Molly, the gown lady. I can hear Papa now; "Two for the price of one, what do you say?" (Now he comes to me: Thank you very much, Papa")

"Well Clara?" He was sitting next to his hyperventilating twenty four year old daughter. "What do you say?"

"What's he look like?" I say. "Does he know what I look like? What does he do?" I went up several decibels. "Damn it Papa, what's his name?"

"His name is Sam, like mine, and he's stopping by Saturday for dinner. Maybe you can borrow the car after and go somewhere to get acquainted." Papa really means business. I unconditionally agreed.

Sam Dayson didn't say much at the house that Saturday evening. Would a composite of Hollywood heartthrobs have to say much? So he was a little thin on top, but the rest of him! I would have needed at least three drinks before imagining some ugly lug half that good looking. He had a gentle way about him and loved the movies. He didn't have a job: They were hard to get. But Sam Dayson did great screen star imitations and Papa could set him up with some kind of work. The wedding went off quite smoothly. I don't know what movie star Sam was when Donny was conceived. He was like some guy doing it by numbers while thinking of what movie he was going to see tomorrow. Sam took to my smother love like he was a package sitting there waiting to be gift-wrapped. He handled my pregnancy with a pat on the tummy and "How you doing, kid?" Kisses became less than cousin-like. Job hunting was trumped by movies and, no doubt, a liaison or three or more.

My Doctor and new friend, Vincent Morante became my confidante. There were more and more appointment extensions that went a bit beyond the professional scene: Mutual admiration ensued. He even helped me do the near impossible: Losing some weight, and keeping it off. I liked myself a lot more and soon after Donny was born, I had the guts to say a quiet farewell to Sam Dayson. I wasn't sure how I felt about Vincent Morante's divorce.

C. HE FOUGHT TO WIN ME: Family

He Fought to Win Me

"Your Grandpa, he fought to win me! You know that Donny? I was a cute little blonde, sixteen years old, and oh how I loved to sing and dance, just like your Aunt Laura and your Momma too."

"Tell me more about Grandpa." I pleaded. "Did he really fight for you?"

I guess I was eight or nine years old the first time Grandma Minnie confided in me like that. Imagine, someone in my own family fighting to win someone else. Grandpa was still around, about ten miles from

Grandma's. They were divorced before I was born, I guess. The matter was not talked about at home. Even my Mom's divorce was never discussed.

Grandpa lived alone in a small apartment, upstairs from the store he operated. People always said he was a handsome, fun-loving man who got along equally well with his men or lady friends. My big events with Grandpa were his short Sunday visits. He'd pinch my cheek, say something quick and nice, and sometimes kiss me so his Sunday stubble scratched but didn't hurt. I liked his soap and cigar smell. He always gave me a piece of Juicy Fruit gum and a quarter for candy and the movies. Grandpa never talked a lot but his visits became more exciting after I became privy to Grandma's piece of family history.

"Your Grandpa used to manage the only ice cream and candy store in town." He worked long hours, I suppose, and I didn't know him, but I used to go in his store with my friends. We sang and laughed and made our soft drinks last a long time. How could I really know him? People who stay in stores were different. They lived somewhere else and didn't have time to sing, dance, and write poems and songs like I did. Yet, he must have known me or he wanted to. I know this because he asked different people about me. He even wrote me a letter in his own hand and had a friend deliver it to me. I answered his letter quickly and told him I was interested in Willy, the cabinet maker's son.

Grandma's head tilted way back, her mouth wide open, her eyes transfixed on the ceiling for a few seconds, then back to my eyes so she could draw me into her fun. She was telling how Grandpa took a day off to find Willy and how he tracked him down in a meat market (sometimes it was in dry goods store) to give him "what for."

Grandma told me many stories. I used to ask her to tell me stories about me. She never let me down, even though she avoided my questions about my father. I knew they were just stories, yet I liked my different roles. How real she made them. Grandma didn't read me any books: She wasn't very good at reading English. Besides, books didn't have the Grandma touch; the backrubs, the chocolate milk, the spirited tunes sung in perfect pitch. The last ten years before Grandma died, our visits had a more distant flavor. Seeing Grandma, or anyone older, became less a pleasure and more of an obligation. I wasn't all that intolerant. I did help Grandma read and write letters. I even listened to, but didn't always appreciate, some of the poems she sent to her special friends and the newspaper. We tuned into the radio: She loved show tunes, classical music and health programs. Sometimes we caught a movie or visited a friend.

I was about nineteen, home for a welcome semester break and holiday, and taking a long ride to Grandma's new apartment. I hadn't seen her for a while and her "health was not good." I had never known her to be ill.

A chilling awareness pulled at my stomach and throat. "What do I do? What do I say?" I smiled a little to myself as I thought of her stories about me, changing frequently to fit the new Donny. I hadn't requested a story for a decade. It had been at least that long since I heard about Grandpa's fight for her. The taut chill returned. My Grandmother was quite sick, maybe dying. I wanted her to be happy; I wanted to see her laugh and hear her sing. I pushed the buzzer to her apartment and straightened the bouquet of mixed flowers in my arm. I waited.

The pungent smell of chicken soup and special dumplings, a few sips of lemonade and some deep breaths warmed and calmed me. Then the question "So how is your Grandpa?" Grandma's moist brown eyes were so soft, yet intense. I thought about forcing a smile or waxing into a nostalgic interlude. Instead I chose, "Oh, he's O.K, pretty busy, I guess."

"Your Grandpa, he fought to win me. You know that Donny?" Grandma retold the story. Although the words seemed quite the same, the impact on me was much more profound. I saw tears traveling down her cheek.

Five days later, I visited Grandpa at his store. I saw an unusually warm intensity in his eyes. "Minnie is gone, Donny."

"I know, Grandpa."

"I didn't hear from her for fifty years and just the other week I got a letter, then in a couple of days, another one. She wanted to get together again, but this time just to talk 'like brother and sister.' When your Grandma writes, it's like poems. You know, I never talked to you about me and Grandma, did I?"

Published: Obelisk, St. Pete College Early 80's

3. Odes, Short Stories

A. A GIRL IN A BLUE DRESS: A Ballad

A girl in a blue dress stands alone by the sea.
Senses gathering quickly what can't seem to be.
Green eyes, they wander from then until now.
Young Summers and Autumns pass her fine brow.

(Soft lips host the salt of the sea, mingling gently.
Focusing now on the rhythm of the rising tide.
Her fingers lift the hem of her flowered blue dress
Just enough to allow the sea to see her twirling dance.)

A red sphere of sunset pushes clouds from her sky
A girl in the blue dress holds a hand on one eye.
Her vista has changed; the moving sea spoken.
What seems joyful and clear is merely a token.

As the sun sinks below and the moon rises high
It sends silver ribbons through the black rippling tide.
The chilled winds of change begin to whip and to blow.
A wizard-like smile then whispers **Hello,**

"I know you, I do!" "The two speak in tandem
Celebrating their meeting occurring at random.
The girl offers her hand, then backs off with fright.
A dozen black ravens blurring her sight.

(The wizard falls into the shadow of the departing birds.
Two of the winged ones remain with the girl.
She watches as they perform their ritual dance of life.
Encircling each other, hardly touching
Then a sudden lunge and they swiftly become one.
They detach in an instant,)

A girl in a blue dress stands alone by the sea.

B. Bedroom

ODE TO ABODE

Thou oft unravished quilt and mattress; Sometimes
A stead of joyful madness.
Now inspected and pawed upon silently, with intent,
by a regal guest, purring, speaking. searching for
Its indented form to rest upon.
The bushy tailed Tabby, quick nap complete
Soars gracefully, her four magical feet landing
On a faux Persian rug piece facing a closeted space
Where outerwear is proudly hanging
Half for thee: Half for me.
Shirts, skirts, color and size coordinated, facing southward
Winter-Autumn-wear hither; Spring-Summer-wear, yon
Top shelf: caps, hats facing southward, every unit vigilant.
Readiness reigns for random inspection.
Feline guide yawns, sweetly calls: Did she utter *'walls?'*
Ah, happy happy walls supporting a panoply of
Memories in picture form: La Plaza del Toro, Grand Canyon
A stroll with Joyce and L. Bloom for a day; Golden Gate; Empire State;
The Coliseum, incompletely perfect, Central Park after dark.
If walls could talk, they'd ask for more: Plenty of room close to the door

Thank you John Keats for inspiration.

C. Chloe in Love

Prologue: This was written by me more than a dozen years ago, following a long distance call from my granddaughter, Chloe, then age 20, telling me about her first 'true love."
I found a rough copy of this recently when looking for something else.
Here is my reaction to the event:

CHLOE, IN LOVE

'Twas the 4th of July two thousand and two
when my soul came attached to eyes, aqua-blue.
The rest of me quivered, sought corners to hide.
Then his voice pierced me softly:
"Please be thou my bride."

A Renaissance Tableaux transcended my mind.
As a dimpled Muse nodded, our fingers entwined.
Propelling us gently to a silent sea.
Our Muse scanned the stars, then let us be.

'Neath us, the sand's gentle bites were inviting
Our voices sang substance in a manner exciting.
Prophets and Poets, some past and some present:
Behold! Fierce Moses, Zen Buddhist, most pleasant
came alive and a part of our sweet clean embrace.
The sea smiled and splashed light salt on our face. .

D. Defining-Confining (Essay)

Defining –Confining- No Exit

Don't define me, don't confine me. Damn it, I am not a stump.
Damn it, I am not a clump. I don't want to stay stuck in an existential dump, left to languish.
People who stay with first impressions frost my rump. I get angry when I catch myself pushing someone into
a confinement box, allowing No Exit, left to languish.
When you point out and say, "You know how _they_ are," I squint out a headache and my throat juices turn
sour. Twisted scripture and other so called truisms are crowded rooms in a smothering cellar.
The very routine boils me when others fall into Defining, Confining.
No Exit-No More

(Short Story:Inspired by THE JEWELS- DeMauppassant)

The day following Emilie Frugaleu's twenty fifth birthday was somewhat tragic, yet it was then that she knew it would soon be time to say farewell to the small country village near Nancy, France.

After Emilie was born in 1845, her father, Henri, vowed to have no more children. An experienced butcher and blacksmith, he was emphatic about training boys and young men exclusively. As years went on and his fine- tuned skills led to increased business, he expanded the geographic area of his work, delivering dressed meats, doing blacksmith work and teaching his trades to young lads. He made a comfortable living. His customer base expanded in spite of his usual 'let's get to business, women are chattel" attitude.

He usually appeared riding his beloved horse and was compared by many of the town-folks to his saddled companion: broad, muscular chest and a proud elongated head. Henri's gait captured the strut of his horse. Yet his countenance lacked the kind softness of the brown-eyed beast.

His wife, Eugenia, from a more cultured yet protected background, continually shuttled between disbelief and disillusionment in the presence of Henri. Her daughter Emilie and she appeared to be the epitome of graceful independence and regal charm. They both chose to forget the marriage of social convenience to Henri, who was outwardly good looking and able to charm Eugenia's parents. Following the birth of Emilie, eye contact and civil conversation were not exchanged between Henri and the ladies. As Emilie grew older and increasingly attractive, not unlike her mother, she often wore a wan and oblivious smile, especially when Henri, after several brandies, ranted about mother and daughter's uselessness and extravagance.

The ladies usually took refuge in the extra room Henri had earlier earmarked for the son who didn't yet appear. Mother and daughter found solace in discussing what could be in their future while deftly manipulating small simple objects and posting instructions for their handicraft in an organized book. Their products became a popular item and mother and daughter exhibited exceptional marketing skills in their locale. One of their best customers was the local jeweler, Lanvin, a recent widower who appeared to continually increase his softly intense eye contact with Emilie.

Comic relief, taking the form of tittering at Henri's ranting, was available daily. Henri, in a rare moment of gauche poetics, compared the ladys' room to their lives: "A place stuck together with paste and little glass pellets, landscaped with people from a world unknown." On days when the brandy flowed freely, Henri proclaimed the room would soon be cleared of all 'this nonsense' and readied for someone who would make his family complete. Following outbursts such as those, Emilie and Eugenia exchanged private smirks and smiles.

Monte Singe was one of M. Frugaleu's prize students. He was eager to learn, quick to agree with his teacher, and his parents paid promptly. During dinner, when Henri was in a more civil mood, he would gloat over M. Singe while gnawing at a large chop. One day he announced, "M. Singe will be our dinner guest next week at this time." Mother and daughter exchanged wry quizzical glances. M. Frugaleu appeared to be touched by sober spirits of composure and industriousness the following six days. He was already setting the table for his favorite student and being quite amenable to wife and daughter. The ladies moved their private lives into boxes and hid them away. Floors were cleaned and repairs, long promised, were completed.

Emilie's languishing hormones were awakened with unexpected anticipation. Henri actually handed some francs to his wife and daughter for new clothing and rich food. M.Frugaleu also lifted the restriction on hot water, more comfortable then for a pleasant bath. He was sharing his domain in a manner Emilie or Eugenia hadn't witnessed for twenty- four years. The ladies still wondered where he kept his francs.

Monte proved to be an attractive dinner guest, employing natural eye contact and smiling head nods to all family members. His age was close to Emilie's. His looks and physique were quite passable, as were his relaxed social graces. For the next several weeks, M. Frugaleu gloated over his new student worker and was even heard humming a Chanson d' Noel. Eugenia and Emilie, not quite ready to join the chorus, spent more time strolling outside in the partly cloudy chill of late fall, exchanging guarded conversation, occasionally sprinkled with spontaneous joy. Monte became a more frequent visitor. Heeding the tacit approval of courtship ritual, he proposed to Emilie. She quietly accepted. They were to marry early December, 1869.

M. Frugaleu's song choices took on a romantic air. He managed to curl his left arm around Monte's broad shoulders and playfully disregarded Emilie's resistance to his outreached right arm. He offered his future son in law a paid apprenticeship in his burgeoning butchering and blacksmith business at 4000 francs a year. Finally that room would be put to good use, at least until the new husband and wife found their own home. Emilie and Eugenia exchanged cautious glances: Could this be a new beginning for their lives as well?

The wedding was a small family gathering. Monte's ailing, albeit well to do, parents struggled to make the trip to the country church. They were observed handing a rather large envelope to their son-their only child- which was then discretely handed to M. Frugaleu. They were pleased that their son found such an agreeable, attractive mate and a most admiring father in law. Eugenia appeared to be happy for her daughter and she repressed any misgivings.

After a few short weeks of pleasurable honeymooning , Monte shed his romantic hide and spent an increasing amount of time with M. Frugaleu, working, drinking and traveling great distances on horseback to accommodate their customers. Eugenia and Emilie soon accepted the fact that this, indeed, was a marriage of obvious convenience. Having M. Frugaleu in a better state of mind was somewhat redeeming, however. While the men were away, the ladies returned to their paste and glass pellets and being quite skilled in horseback riding, went to nearby villages where they developed an active business. Most of their profits were carefully layered in a well-disguised compartment where their materials were stored.

There was a rather generous exchange of gifts for Christmas: household goods for the ladies, shoes, tools and basic clothing for the men. Just when everyone thought the gift giving was completed, M. Frugaleu slipped into the basement and returned with a bulky, hastily wrapped package and, with the brightest of smiles, presented it to Monte. It was a replica of a piece of clothing he had crafted for himself out of horsehide many years ago. Eugenie and Emilie called it his 'second hide,' for he was seldom seen without it on his back. The roughly made coat had two deep slit pockets, nearly invisible to the casual onlooker. Monte embraced his father in law midst happy tears.

Emilie and Eugenia were peering out the window one early morning, the first week of January. They could barely discern the dark brown silhouettes on horseback, slowly dissolving into a very large gray cloud.

"They are one in mind and body, especially now that they are wearing those homely coats," said Emilie, with a droll tremolo in her voice.

"Well mother, we do have a busy day planned, don't we? Besides, I have an early morning appointment with Dr. Chamagne. My mornings have been less than comfortable lately."

Eugenia revealed a new smile. "Ah yes, dear, there is work to do and finally we get to go the theatre. The players from a nearby university are working hard to give our town some culture. Still, we should be home before the men. They have a long day and will most certainly stop at M. Benoit's tavern to celebrate something. Let's get a move on, for the coach will be here for us soon. I hope the sun shines a bit."

The day did brighten, although ominous clouds returned as mother and daughter joyfully purchased theatre tickets early evening. They had a marvelous time laughing through Moliere's "Tartuffe," especially during the 'hair shirt' scene. Somehow it reminded them of their two men suffering under cumbersome coats all year long. They stopped at a little tea shoppe after the show, still raving about their new, favorite play and promising it would not be the last. Their shared dreams of visiting Paris were accompanied by the percussive beats of the sturdy carriage horses. What a glorious birthday present this had been for Emilie!

It must have been three o'clock the next morning that mother and daughter were awakened by the tavern owner, M. Benoit, and a police officer. They escorted the ladies to a dark scene: There were two riderless horses draped with heavy, coarse coats across their saddle .

"They must have been struck by lightning outside the tavern, Madame. Their lives ended on the way to the hospital." The gentlemen spoke in tandem and expressed their regrets.

Emilie and Eugenia froze for a moment, embraced and allowed little moist tears to fall on their cheeks. They thanked the gentlemen and said they would ride into town in the morning and take care of the arrangements. M. Benoit and the officer bowed deeply and departed.

An uncontrollable storm of genuine tears poured from the ladys'eyes as they removed the heavy coats from the jittery horses. The knowing mares nuzzled the widows' faces and gently nudged the homely hides in the general direction of the hidden slit pockets. The ladies began a casual search. Eugenia was the first to speak.

"Mon Dieu! so many books, receipts and...Look at this!" Emilie and Eugenia reared their heads and emitted a high pitched shriek, then a choking, close to hysterical, chortle: "They carried their banks on their backs!" uttered Emilie, shaking her head and smiling in disbelief.

Three weeks passed: The ladies departed from their 'place stuck together with paste and little glass pellets' except for taking a few sentimental mementos Emilie decided to save.

Dr. Chamagne confirmed what mother and daughter expected to hear: A new baby was on its way. They found a new home in the suburbs of Paris to their liking and comfortably settled in the picturesque locale near the Cultural Center.

Emilie found her husband, M. Lantin, the charming widower and jeweler whose four year old daughter Jacqueline, was pleased to have a younger baby sister, Brigitte. Eugenia served as a model mother in law and watchful grandmother. The new romantic atmosphere caught hold of her and she had no problem attracting dashing town squires, one of whom she soon married and they moved a few kilometers from Emilie and family.

M.Lantin mocked complaining when Emilie, in a teasing fashion, sometimes chose to wear those paste and pellet mementos when they frequented fancy restaurants, theatre, opera and other glorious sites of nearby Paris. Yet, she allowed herself to love and adore him as she did no other. M.Lantin's love for her accelerated as the years flew by.

Emilie eventually trashed the paste and pellet combinations and agreed to occasionally wear unobtrusive pieces of genuine high end jewelry from her vast collection purchased earlier from the merchant on the corner of Rue de la Paix near Nancy, France.

G. Letter to Enrique: Reflections of a Retired Lit. Professor

Enrique;

I found an address of yours on a Christmas card from nine years ago. Maybe you are still living there. Just like the rest of your family, you included a note with the "poor me" routine. I hate being used. I don't get any personal mail or family visitors: That is OK by me. So, why do I write to you?

Is it the Feast Day? I don't think so. Nor am I mellowing out now that I reached "three score +ten." This do-gooder gnat named Pedro told me I better get in touch with family, that's why. He manages to visit me several times a week, whether I like it or not. If he didn't carry institutional burritos or enchiladas up those rotting four steps, I wouldn't open the door for him either.

Once he gets inside, he does his 'brighten up' routine, opening windows, pulling up shades and straightening out all over my place. Then he chides me for being a hermit and says to get out of my "crappy cave." It's bad enough I have to listen to yelping dogs or squealing kids and their drunken parents in this beaten converted bodega in a 'burg' the City of Angels would rather not claim. He even took me to Rodeo Drive one afternoon and tried to impress me, waving at those Hollywood has-beens.

One afternoon he spotted me in the back yard pushing a shopping cart I took from the grocer's parking lot. I told him it was my Walker; it helps me get around better. When he asked me why I was carting gasoline cans, I told him to mind his own business and go back to Mexico with the other 'wetbacks.' He smiled.

Not only does this Happy Face test the purity of la lengua materna-the mother tongue- he tries to get into my intellectual good graces. He wants to talk about those pagan ceremonies on Olvera Street and to really get to me; he browses through my library. "Mind if I borrow <u>A HUNDRED YEARS OF SOLITUDE</u>" for a couple of weeks," he asked one day.

Then he tried to get real chummy with his Echo Park pseudointellectual banter: "I just finished <u>"Like Water for Chocolate"</u> by Laura Esquival: Didn't she borrow from Marquez?" That's when I threw Mr. Happy Gnat out of my house. He better get that book back to me quickly! That's enough for now. You don't have to write back.

Your Papa

H. LOBBY MEETING

Lobby Meeting .
Short Story

The two of them walked into the lobby, led by a six pound fluffy poodle type, with "Westminster First Prize" etched in her gait. The lady on the other end of the jeweled leash didn't have to bend too far to pick up her pet. Both appeared to have just departed from their respective beauty salons and shared a clean, captivating essence. The lady was a candidate for a fully clothed Victoria's Secret model.

A building of a man toying with an aromatic cheroot between two massive digits was a foot or two behind them. He was a blend of disinterest and mild disgust. His voice, registering high pitch, pointed at the poodle; "Hey Tinkerbell, park your invisible butt, before I park it for you. "The man's attractive features were masked by his strident sound and oversized dark glasses. The demure lady reddened as she glanced at me, then to a younger blonde man who had just entered the lobby. He sat six feet across from the couple and pulled out a magazine. The lady's stage whisper was barely audible: Her stare was caked with a sneer. She spoke:

"You know her name is Cheri and please keep your voice down." The lady and Cheri softly exchanged a few phrases and she offered me and the blonde man a head shake and a wan smile.

The big man's other hand was sparring with a full cup of coffee, asking waves and spilling intermittently on the plush crimson at his feet. His gaze zoomed through me and aimed at the blonde man. "You finding this picture amusing, Mr. Smiley Face?" He removed his dark glasses and hardened his stare. "You think I like trailing behind this excuse for a dog? I didn't ask for this ball of nothing: Hmmf; 'Some gift from a distant relative.' Good thing it's a distant one." The big man put on his dark glasses, put the cheroot in his mouth and announced; " I am going out for a change of scenery and a smoke."

The lobby was quiet. Cheri decided to socialize, allowed me to pet her, then to the young blonde man, who spoke to the poodle in a familiar manner; "So good to see you again: You have a new name. What a pretty one you are." He cradled Cheri and carried her, walking toward the lady and sat next to her. Her stage whisper was barely audible; "Thank you for the lovely present. Cheri and I will see you again."

I. MATT AND MARCY

MATT AND MARCY

Short Story

Marcy's nondescript humming midst a cadence of knitting needles rubbing together creates the scenario. Nearby, an outside door opens and Matt enters, focuses on Marcy, tilts his head and speaks:

Matt: "I'm back. Baby sitter is home safely. She had an early night. You feeling OK?"

Marcy: " Yeah" (Close to inaudible) Humming stops; Knitting needles quicken the cadence.

Marcy's focus follows the stretching dog on the floor next to her.

Matt: "What's with the pissy attitude, Marcy? You sure made it known you wanted to leave early."

Marcy: (Volume increases, tears in her voice. "Do you really care?"

Matt: (Shakes head) "Hey c'mon; Not again." His nostrils flare and lips tighten.

Marcy: (She hesitates, wipes her nose, looks up and says,) "Why can't you act like a normal person instead of some jerk?" (Her eyes, now dry, are squinting.)

Matt: (Responds quickly and more vocal) "Screw normal. When do you decide to pay me a compliment? Some people do and you get so ticked off: I can see it." (His neck muscles are taut.)

Marcy: (Harrumphs and picks up the small terrier at her side, sweetly cooing,) "What are we going to do with your Daddy?"

The next ten minutes is fraught with rhetorical questions: ("When will you ever grow up?" Have you ever thought about going for therapy? Why do you insist upon grabbing the spotlight? When are you going to stop making up those lies at my expense? Can't you see they don't believe you?)"

Matt: (Following a brief silence.) "Isn't it cute when you turn the dog against me."

Marcy: "Aren't you the big man driving our kids to resent me.?" (Telephone rings in next room. Marcy picks up the phone. Her mouth opens and eyes widen.) . "What a treat, mother, to hear from you. Sure, stop by. Matt and I were wondering how you are. We were just fixing a drink and there are enough goodies for you and Dad."

Marcy: "Guess who is coming for a drink." She strokes her dog and places the phone down gently.

J. MISS JANE

MISS JANE Short Story

Prologue

Having just finished proof reading the last paragraph of my English Literature thesis, I find myself stuck, not wanting to depart from the main character of my paper, Jane Austen. I gaze at the half-empty bottle before me.

Chardonnay, cheap Chardonnay, lingers and battles high-octane peppermints lolling on my pale tongue. My eyes close and flicker while I try to reconstruct THE VISIT. I'm gently fingering a slippery book cover and chuckling, somewhat sadly. A melancholy mist is crawling about my temple.

The Visit

I was swapping appropriate kisses and wild hugs and growls with Pugalicious, my blonde and tan Pug, when I heard a knock at the front door. Hardly anyone comes to our front door. Pugalicious maintained the beat with a chortle, the likes of which I had never heard. Gingerly, I opened the door and allowed a sew-capped silhouette to enter. She spoke softly.

Her voice was like a charming cello, beckoning, yet subdued enough to subtly entice. I found myself gently holding her hand and placing my other arm around her waist, then dancing an eighteenth century polka.

Just as I began adjusting my focus on this ethereal stature, she handed me a book exuding aromatic leather, its cover, slippery smooth. A flowered note fell from the book. I read it.

"When you open this book, you will open your life to me and to you."

My fingers clasped and lingered on my visitor's warm hands and I imagined (or did I?) her lips gently brushing my ear.

She whispered, "Read me slowly, slowly: Allow yourself to know the depths of me,Behold my knowing winks, reserved for you who refuse to just skim me. When you read me. I want only you holding my soft, sometimes slippery self."

The visit took on a crescendo of a clanging beacon and cut through the smog in my temple and chest. I wanted to be with her. I found another handwritten note in my unexpected gift, "It is a universal truth that those expecting good fortune may receive it in a most unexpected manner." "Oh yes! This is her style." I exclaimed. "I must be with her."

Pugalicious jumped upon my lap and nuzzled the richness of the book's cover. She pushed our new glistening gift to the floor with her soft nose and jumped upon the book gently. When I went to pick it up, she nudged me away and began rubbing the buttery book surface with her own warm, welcoming, damp bottom. The redolence of a rich cologne and Pugalicious's yearning femininity meshed. During this encounter, I noticed more writing on the other side of the paper. My body shivered as I read its contents.

Here in my shaking hand was the letter I had recently sent to **Cordial Coupling Services requesting information about the possibility of breeding my beloved dog. My teeth clattered at high intensity as I scanned to the bottom of the note. Written in a feminine eighteenth century** quill-script was the following: 'Please do request Homer.' Our guest departed. Pugalicious and I had a fitful sleep.

We jumped in the truck early the next morning and headed for the Coupling Service in the teeth of a storm.

A thunderclap increased my anxiety. The Jeep radio serenaded us with a rollicking Mozart Overture. The hills were alive with the sound of canine coupling. We arrived, leapt out of the truck and raced toward the reception area, Pugalicious jumped and yelped, huffing all the way.

Lightning struck a nearby tree and a diminutive figure appeared briefly near a fallen branch. I heard a calming Cello Sonata accompanying this passing event.

The storm blew over quickly as the owner of the establishment greeted us in her office. After filling out the necessary papers and presenting my pug's credentials, I made it a point to request Homer. The owner laughed and gazed at the ceiling.

"You must have been speaking to our Miss Jane", she said. "Jane can always sense a perfect match . Well, look who is here to greet us."

EPILOGUE

Pugalicious and Homer fell in love at first glow and produced a fantastic litter; My sweet pug's final voyage to motherhood. I am still not certain if the Miss Jane who came through that door was the same silhouette that visited us. She surely did 'sense some perfect matches.' Jane loves me to read to her while she strokes Pugalicious and her puppy, Austen.

ONE LAST DANCE Poem

A single nymph revolves slowly around a spire.
A lush rainbow of silk
faithfully follows each move
of the soft, marble body.
I reach toward the twirling figure
hundreds of yards above me.

She flicks her tongue in fun.
As a final insult,
she expends a surge of energy
Rockets downward.
My longing arms extend,

One last dance, my love?

Night falls and beckons the final performance.
My fantasy of Eden dissolves,
save for a tatter of shimmering silk wrapped around my sagging shoulders.

Short Story

Resolution and irony greeted me and my daughter, Maria, one rainy Saturday. We were waiting on a slow-moving express line in the neighborhood super market. I don't get to see Maria as much as I'd like. She's a bright, busy twenty-five- year old living on her own. I've been a single parent for about twenty years.

"Hey Mom," she spoke in a high whisper, "Check the line crasher in front of us. She not only cut us off and swung into the express lane; she had at least twenty items in her basket." "Now listen to her, bitching about the narrow aisles and the changed displays." Maria and I tried to quietly ignore this lack of super market ethics. The offender did a sudden about face. Our chins dropped.

"I thought I recognized your voices," a guttural snarl barked from her throat. Our three step move backwards was involuntary.

"That's Sammy's Bird lady," we lip-synched. She approached us in slow motion.

Flash back Fourteen Years:

We, Maria and I, were living in a middle class, residential, second floor walkup, a rustic area in West Central Florida. There were plenty of birds, squirrels and some lazy, chubby cats nearby, who steered clear of an exotic visitor, often accompanied by a homeschooled young lad of ten or so. Everyone called him Sammy.

Sammy's proud Peacock companion, named Rainbow, sometimes followed, sometimes led the young boy.

Most of us neighborhood people exchanged cordial greetings with the unusual, yet colorful, duo. An accompanying musical cadence was easy to imagine.

Sammy's Mom, although not seen as often, occasionally made a special visit to our home and presented us with a gorgeous feather, compliments of Rainbow. I think Mom's name was Bernadette.

"Call me Birdie," she said at our first meeting. Birdie's favorite topics were Rainbow and, of course, Sammy. Maria and I looked forward to Birdie's visits, not only because of the decorative feathers we received. It was a special treat for us to see Birdie's proud smile and puffed out chest while she spoke. Her apparel was often color coordinated with the peacock's plumage. Birdie always presented new or old, always entertaining, anecdotes involving their special family. The trio was a unique and welcome part of our amiable neighborhood, that is, with one exception: She whom we called, with not a minimum of sarcasm, Sammy's Bird Lady.

I really don't recall her proper name. We called her Tillie. It was Tillie who scoffed at Sammy when he and Rainbow strutted down the dirt road in our shared, unfenced back yard. "Go on you little Pantywaist, you and that dirty screeching bird." Sammy's clothing was a mélange of splashed bright paints. Tillie yelled, "You're starting to look more and more like brothers." Her frozen scowl was accentuated by a lighted cigarette hanging from her bottom lip, and three or four dangling chin hairs. A wrinkled loose fitting housedress wrapped itself around a bony figure. Tillie did try to get the rest of us neighbors to sign her protest, even to the point of her getting a petition drawn up to keep that bird off of our property. No success.

Sammy's Bird Lady and her seldom seen male live in companion soon became almost invisible in our neighborhood, except for the screams between them and Tillie's occasional outbursts when Sammy and friend strutted by. The boy and his pet seldom heeded the plaintive Tillie. That is, until one spring morning as Maria and I were rushing down the steps to our back yard, in search of the source of gruesome sounds below.

We were harshly struck by a surreal skirmish and became part of what I imagined to be the overcrowded halls of hysterical Hades. Rainbow was writhing and rolling, his bloodied feathers flying, trying to escape the grunting Tillie, swinging a shovel above him. Sammy, helplessly crawling to and from the ruckus, screamed, "My beautiful bird: My best friend."

Two police officers swung out of their Sheriff's vehicle and moved cautiously toward the scenario. Tillie tossed away her shovel and ran to her apartment. Birdie carried the limp Peacock under her arm and guided Sammy away from the battleground. Maria and I were seated on the bottom step, shaking and sobbing. We soon moved away and never returned to that memorable neighborhood, although we played the scene many times and many ways. Tillie usually got top billing. On occasion, we shamelessly mocked her, midst loud laughter. Now she is leering at us on a rainy Saturday morning on the express line in our neighborhood market. "I didn't hurt that bird and you reported me. It was my roommate: He drove me crazy. They put me away for a long time." Tillie inched closer to us.

"You reported me." The phrase echoed in my mind.

"No Tillie, I never reported you. I remember you accusing me fourteen years ago as you were running toward your house. I hear your angry words every day; I am so sorry." I felt Maria's hand on my shoulder.

Tillie's face took on an unfamiliar glow: She breathed deeply and smiled just a bit. She had a freshproduce allure. "It's OK; I have already forgiven you and everyone else, including myself." Our hands joined each other's briefly. Maria gently massaged my neck. Years of confusing fear and moments of mockery slowly dissolved. A cheerful checkout lady greeted us. "Did you find everything all right?"

Published: The Binnacle-University of Maine at Machias

M. SHE JOYFULLY RUNS

Poem-Some Haiku Style

Prologue
Haiku:
"Murmur, heartbeat slow
Does she cough?" Sad self shakes No
"She joyfully runs."

She joyfully runs, paying heed to onlookers
Sometimes slowing to comfortably chat.

She joyfully runs, taking lead with no hubris
Making small talk with a neighborly cat.

She joyfully runs, giving face kisses galore
Reading our plans; when we eat, when we sleep.

Now I wait by the phone for her Doctor's report
Pick up on second ring. "She's good." Hearts leap.

Epilogue
Haiku:
One month flashes by
Now her joyful runs on earth
Seek peace in heaven.
Published: The Binnacle-University of Maine, at Machias

About the Author:

Thanks to his grandmother, whom he has given recognition to in his writings, his favorite aunt, wife and a couple of English professors, Don has been writing and teaching at St. Pete College more than forty years. Following a BA in Sociology and English as well as an MA in Special Education, he was nominated by St. Petersburg College as Professor Emeritus-Human Services. Don has been published by The Binnacle, University of Maine at Machias, St. Petersburgh Times, The Obelisk, St. Petersburgh Junior College.

Printed in the United States
By Bookmasters